THE LOVE ONE ANOTHE

HONORING
HOLDING OTHERS IN HIGH REGARD

A Bible Study by

Churches Alive!

MINISTERING TO THE CHURCHES OF THE WORLD
600 Meridian Avenue, Suite 200
San Jose, California 95126-3427

Published by

BRINGING TRUTH TO LIFE
NavPress Publishing Group
P.O. Box 35001, Colorado Springs, Colorado 80935

Because we share kindred aims for helping local churches fulfill Christ's Great Commission to "go and make disciples," NavPress and Churches Alive have joined efforts on certain strategic publishing projects that are intended to bring effective disciplemaking resources into the service of the local church.

For more than a decade, Churches Alive has teamed up with churches of all denominations to establish vigorous disciplemaking ministries. At the same time, NavPress has focused on publishing Bible studies, books, and other resources that have grown out of The Navigators' 50 years of disciplemaking experience.

Now, together, we're working to offer special products like this one that are designed to stimulate a deeper, more fruitful commitment to Christ in the local gatherings of His Church.

The LOVE ONE ANOTHER *series was written by Russ Korth, Ron Wormser, Jr., and Ron Wormser, Sr. of Churches Alive. Many individuals from both Churches Alive and NavPress contributed greatly in bringing this project to publication.*

Contents

Honoring people with your actions without an attitude of respect is not really honoring them at all. True honor involves both right attitudes and right actions.

Seeing Value in Others

▼

1 In society, what systems of evaluation do people use to establish value in others?

2 What is the true value of believers who may appear to be of lesser value? (1 Corinthians 12:22-25)

3 What intrinsic value is in all people? (Genesis 1:26-27)

4 What value has God given people? (Psalm 8:3-8)

5 How did Jesus express the value He saw in Peter and Nathaniel? (John 1:42-48)

6 Do you usually feel that Jesus sees value in you? Why, or why not?

7 What was Jesus' evaluation of the value of John the Baptist? (Luke 7:24-28)

8 What are some practical ways you can see more value in people than the intrinsic value God has given all people?

9 a. Read Esther 6. Why did the king see value in Mordecai? Why didn't Haman see value in Mordecai?

b. What lessons from this passage can be applied to society today?

10 What are some of the things that happen when you see value in others?

Honoring Leaders

▼

1 Write a short paragraph telling what it means to honor someone.

2 Whom should you honor? (1 Peter 2:17)

3 Complete the chart.

CHARACTERISTICS LEADING TO HONOR	AN EXAMPLE OF A LEADER WITH THIS CHARACTERISTIC	HOW TO GAIN THIS CHARACTERISTIC
Proverbs 15:33		
Proverbs 20:3		
Proverbs 21:21		
Proverbs 22:4		

4 What kind of leader does God honor?

1 Samuel 2:30

Isaiah 66:1-2

5 What is an improper use of honor? (James 2:1-4)

6 a. First Peter 2:17 says you are to honor the king. Who do you think are your "kings" today?

b. What are some things you can do to honor them?

Matthew 22:17-21

1 Timothy 2:1-3

7 a. Who is to be honored, according to 1 Timothy 6:1-2?

    b. What would be a modern-day parallel to this relationship?

    c. How can honor be shown in this relationship?

8 a. Who is to be honored, according to 1 Thessalonians 5:12-13?

b. What is one important way to do this?
  (1 Timothy 5:17-18)

c. Name those who are over you in the Lord.

9 What are some other ways to honor leaders in your church?

10 Read 1 Samuel 24. How can you follow the example of David in honoring a leader?

Lesson Three
Honoring Family Members

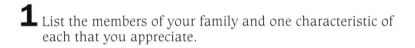

1 List the members of your family and one characteristic of each that you appreciate.

2 a. What principle about honor is stated in John 4:44?

b. In your opinion, why is this true?

3 a. What is commanded in Exodus 20:12?

b. How is the importance of this command shown in Exodus 21:15,17?

4 a. What is the difference between honoring parents and obeying parents?

b. Write down one specific thing you plan to do this week that will honor your parent(s). (Be prepared to share your experience with the group.)

5 What can parents do to honor their children? (2 Corinthians 12:14)

6 Moses honored Joshua in Numbers 27:18-23. Though theirs was not a parent-child relationship, how can you as a parent honor your children in a similar way?

7 What does 1 Peter 3:7 teach about husbands honoring their wives?

8 What are some things wives can do to honor their husbands? (Titus 2:4-5)

9 a. What are some of the long-range effects of a lack of honor in the family?

   b. What are some of the long-range effects of honor in the family?

Putting others first does not mean always putting them at the front of the line. It means giving their interests higher priority than your own.

Deferring to Others

▼

1 Holding a door open for someone is a little thing that defers to another. What are some other common ways we defer to one another on a daily basis?

2 Why should you defer to others? (Philippians 2:1-4)

3 Study Matthew 5:38-42.

a. Briefly describe the old principle. (Verse 38)

b. Briefly describe the new principle. (Verse 39)

c. How did Jesus apply this new principle to each of these situations?

■ Being sued in court.

■ Being forced to help someone.

■ Being asked to lend to someone.

4 Study Matthew 5:43-48.

a. Briefly describe the old principle. (Verse 43)

b. Briefly describe the new principle. (Verse 44)

c. How did Jesus illustrate the new principle in verse 45?

d. Whom are you like if you don't apply this principle? (Verses 46-47)

e. Whom are you like if you do apply this principle? (Verse 48)

5 What reasons did Jesus give for applying the principles studied in questions 3 and 4 to your life? (Luke 6:46-49)

6 a. Give an example of when the command of 1 Corinthians 10:24 would not include deferring to another.

b. What do you think is the proper action to take in the situation you described?

7 Your neighbor continually borrows tools from you. Usually they are not returned unless you ask for them, and then they are dirty and rusty. How would you apply the teaching of this chapter in your dealings with your neighbor?

8 In the passages below are situations where people either did or did not put others first. Choose one situation to meditate upon this week and write out the most important lesson you learn about putting others first.

☐ Abraham dividing the land with Lot (Genesis 13:5-13)
☐ Jacob dealing with Esau (Genesis 25:29-34)
☐ The story of Esther (book of Esther)
☐ The centurion's servant being healed (Luke 7:2-10)
☐ The good Samaritan (Luke 10:25-37)

9 Does putting others first mean that you have to say and do what they want? Explain.

Jesus taught to esteem others by serving them
in ways they don't expect.

LESSON FIVE
Serving Others
▼

1 a. Name a contemporary person whom you would enjoy serving.

b. Why would serving that person be enjoyable while serving others might not be?

2 Study Matthew 20:20-28.

a. What did James, John, and their mother request of Jesus?

b. Did Jesus indicate that there was anything wrong with their ambition? Explain your answer.

c. In your opinion, why were the other ten disciples indignant?

d. Knowing their desire, what did Jesus say they should do?

3 Study John 13:1-17.

a. When in Jesus' life did this event take place?

b. What significance do you attach to this timing?

c. What principle do you think Jesus was teaching to His disciples?

d. Jesus taught this principle to the fellowship of the Twelve. How can this be applied today in your fellowship?

4 a. What is the main point of Jesus' teaching in Luke 17:7-10? (KJV—"trow" = "think")

b. How does this principle apply to a person who wants appreciation and recognition for his church work?

5 a. List at least five important characteristics of service found in Ephesians 6:5-7.

b. What is promised in Ephesians 6:8?

6 Read the account of Abraham's servant in Genesis 24. List at least three characteristics of this servant's life and tell how they are demonstrated.

CHARACTERISTIC	HOW DEMONSTRATED
Singleminded	*He didn't let anything deter or delay him.*

7 Why should wholeheartedness characterize all endeavors of Christians? (Colossians 3:23-24)

8 a. If you were a servant, why would you find the instructions of 1 Peter 2:18 difficult to obey? (KJV—"froward" = "unreasonable")

b. Describe a current situation to which you feel this verse applies.

9 a. In your own words, relate the principle that Jesus gives in Luke 16:10.

b. How can you apply this principle as you consider your responsibilities in your church? See also Luke 16:11.

10 a. What is one reason God has given you freedom in Christ? (Galatians 5:13)

b. Give an example of how you can use your freedom to serve others.

c. How can you have power to serve one another? (Galatians 5:16)

11 a. What principle does Paul present in Galatians 6:7?

b. How does he apply this principle to serving others? (Galatians 6:9-10)

Humility is not the art of thinking poorly of yourself.
Humility involves a true evaluation of yourself, seeing both
your strengths and weaknesses. With a correct view
of yourself, you can esteem others properly.

Humility Before God

▼

1 a. In what ways is a pet's relationship to its master like a humble relationship to God?

b. What might cause many people to resent being compared to a pet?

2 What characteristics are associated with humility before God?

Psalm 69:30-32

Psalm 131:1-3

3 Why can you say humility does not require a continual sense of guilt? (Colossians 2:13-14)

4 Rewrite Micah 6:8 in your own words.

5 Why should you be humble before God? (Romans 9:20-21)

6 What are some of the blessings God promises to people who are humble?

Psalm 10:17

Isaiah 57:15

Matthew 5:5

7 What are some of the actions associated with humility before God? (2 Corinthians 7:14)

8 What are some obstacles you see to being humble before God?

9 Write a short letter to God telling Him how you feel about walking humbly with Him.

10 a. Read Psalm 23. In what ways is David describing a humble walk with God?

b. If you did not like the earlier comparison of a pet and its master, how do you feel about the comparison of a sheep and a shepherd?

Humility Before Others

▼

1 a. Play the "That's Nothing" game by writing a fictitious ending to the response below with an extreme boast.

"I won the Pulitzer Prize for literature."
"That's nothing. I . . ."

b. What happens in relationships when people play the "That's Nothing" game without tongue in cheek?

2 What characteristics are associated with humility before others?

Matthew 18:4

Ephesians 4:2-3

Philippians 2:1,4

3 Jesus' actions were never inconsistent with true humility. How does His example show the following concepts to be false?

"Humility means never making offensive statements." (Matthew 15:7-12)

"Humility means never acting confidently." (Mark 1:21-22)

"Humility means being passive in all situations." (John 2:13-17)

"Humility means never saying anything positive about yourself." (John 8:12-14)

4 Philippians 2:5-11 describes Jesus' humility. Briefly describe His thoughts and His actions and the results of them.

5 a. The passages below relate two similar experiences. Compare Jesus' responses in these two situations. How are they different? How are they the same?

Luke 9:46-48

Luke 22:24-27

b. What do you conclude from studying these passages?

6 a. What does 1 Peter 5:5-6 teach about your relationship to others in your church?

b. Give the names of some to whom you should apply this teaching.

7 a. What is one way lack of humility reveals itself? (Matthew 6:1)

b. What are some current ways people violate Jesus' teaching in Matthew 6:1?

8 What principle did Jesus teach in Luke 14:7-11?

9 a. Imagine a banquet. Someone is sitting in the guest of honor's seat. The host asks him to move so that the guest of honor can sit down. Put yourself in the position of each of the following people and briefly describe how you would feel.

■ The host.

■ The guest of honor.

■ The person being asked to move.

■ One of the other people attending the banquet.

b. Now imagine another banquet. The guest of honor arrives and takes a seat. The host approaches him and asks him to come to the head table to take the seat of honor. Again put yourself in the place of each person present and briefly describe how you would feel.

■ The host.

■ The guest of honor.

■ One of the other people attending the banquet.

c. What insight did you gain from the preceding exercises?

10 a. Read 2 Kings 5:1-16. How do you see humility or lack of it demonstrated in the life of Naaman?

b. What do you conclude about humility from studying this example?

11 a. Which works of the flesh listed in Galatians 5:19-21 do you associate with a lack of humility?

b. Which characteristics of the fruit of the Spirit listed in Galatians 5:22-23 do you associate with humility?

c. How then can you be humble? (Galatians 5:25-26)

12 Give some of the advantages you see to being humble.

There are times when everyone is eager to learn. Being truly teachable means maintaining this attitude continually.

When you esteem others, you want to learn all you can from them.

Learning from Others

▼

1 Who was your best teacher during high school? What made him or her the best?

2 From the benefits of learning named in Proverbs 1:1-6, list the three that are most important to you and tell why.

3 What can help you to learn from others?

Proverbs 20:5

1 Corinthians 8:2

James 1:19

4 a. From whom should you learn?

Proverbs 10:31

Proverbs 13:20

b. Name some of the people from whom you personally can learn.

5 What should accompany learning? (Philippians 4:9)

6 What steps of learning do you see in Proverbs 24:30-34?

7 a. Read Acts 17:10-11. What actions accompanied the Bereans' teachability?

   b. Why?

   c. What can you as an individual do to copy these activities at your church's worship services?

8 What are some of the things another person might do if he or she thinks you have an unteachable attitude?

Job 32:1-2

Matthew 10:14

9 Describe how a teachable attitude, or lack of it, has affected your relationship with another person.

10 What helps you learn from Sunday morning sermons?

Accepting Correction

▼

---

1 a. What qualifications should you have before offering correction to another?

b. What qualifications should another have before you accept correction from them?

2 Why should you be teachable in accepting reproof?

Proverbs 15:5

Proverbs 15:31-32

Proverbs 29:1

3 If a person who reproves you is following Proverbs 9:8-9, what is his or her evaluation of you?

4 What does 1 Peter 2:20 indicate you should do if you are reproved wrongly? (KJV—"buffeted" = "beaten")

5 Describe a situation where you benefited from reproof.

6 a. Read Galatians 2:11-14. What adjectives would you use to describe Paul's correction of Peter?

b. Describe a situation in which this type of correction would be appropriate today.

7 Sometimes "correction" is based on false teaching instead of truth. What will help you identify false teachers?

Matthew 7:15-20

1 John 4:1-6

8 Read 2 Peter 2 and list something you observe in each of the categories below.

What false teachers teach

The character of false teachers

The actions of false teachers

The effects of false teachers

The end of false teachers

What false teachers are like

NOTES AND PRAYER REQUESTS

NOTES AND PRAYER REQUESTS

NOTES AND PRAYER REQUESTS

NOTES AND PRAYER REQUESTS

If you enjoyed this study, you'll want to check out the other titles in the LOVE ONE ANOTHER series:

SMALL-GROUP MATERIALS FROM NAVPRESS

BIBLE STUDY SERIES

CRISISPOINTS FOR WOMEN
DESIGN FOR DISCIPLESHIP
GOD IN YOU
GOD'S DESIGN FOR THE FAMILY
INSTITUTE OF BIBLICAL
   COUNSELING SERIES

LIFECHANGE
LIFESTYLE SMALL GROUP SERIES
LOVE ONE ANOTHER
STUDIES IN CHRISTIAN LIVING
THINKING THROUGH DISCIPLESHIP

TOPICAL BIBLE STUDIES

Becoming a Woman of
   Excellence
Becoming a Woman of Freedom
The Blessing Study Guide
Celebrating Life
Growing in Christ
Growing Strong in God's Family
Homemaking
Intimacy with God

Loving Your Husband
Loving Your Wife
A Mother's Legacy
Surviving Life in the Fast Lane
To Run and Not Grow Tired
To Walk and Not Grow Weary
What God Does When Men Pray
When the Squeeze Is On

BIBLE STUDIES WITH COMPANION BOOKS

Bold Love
From Bondage to Bonding
Hiding from Love
Inside Out
The Masculine Journey
The Practice of Godliness
The Pursuit of Holiness

Secret Longings of the
   Heart
Transforming Grace
Trusting God
What Makes a Man?
The Wounded Heart
Your Work Matters to God

RESOURCES

Curriculum Resource Guide
How to Lead Small Groups
Jesus Cares for Women
The Small Group Leaders
   Training Course

Topical Memory System (KJV/NIV
   and NASB/NKJV)
Topical Memory System: Life
   Issues (KJV/NIV and
   NASB/NKJV)

VIDEO PACKAGES

Abortion
Bold Love
Hope Has Its Reasons
Inside Out

Living Proof
Parenting Adolescents
Unlocking Your Sixth Suitcase
Your Home, A Lighthouse

This study is just one item in a wide range of small group material authored by Churches Alive. Continue your study with other books in this series.

Churches Alive has local representatives who provide their own living expenses to serve you at your church. On-site support and training conferences will develop commitment and vision in group leaders. Our experienced staff can help you develop leaders, enrich your groups, and reach out to others.

Conferences and Support Services

Conferences

A Pastor's Perspective:

"Churches Alive was a tremendous help to us when we were getting started in our discipleship ministry. We had to make a choice—either try to learn ourselves and make a lot of mistakes, or get some help and minimize mistakes. Their careful but goal-oriented approach helps any church build a solid, perpetuating ministry."

Designed to strengthen the effectiveness of your leaders, our conferences and seminars range from one to four days. Most are taught by Churches Alive staff and local pastors. In addition, we arrange special seminars in your church to encourage people in your church to study the Bible.

Support Services

In dozens of denominations, our staff helps churches large and small. We can help you evaluate, plan, train leaders, and expand your small groups. Invite a Churches Alive representative to explore small group discipleship at your church.

Churches Alive!
600 Meridian Avenue
Suite 200
San Jose, CA 95126
(408) 294-6000
(408) 294-6029 FAX

Call 1-800-755-3787